HERO DAD MINDSET

HOW TO PREPARE FOR AND WIN AT FATHERHOOD

PETER BLACK

DEDICATION

For L, thank you for giving me the chance to be someone's hero

INTRODUCTION

Being a father can be one of the most enjoyable and rewarding experiences in a man's life. But, it can be one of the most stressful roles too. This book will walk you through all of the changes you can expect, and how best to navigate those changes that await you as you enter fatherhood. Your life is going to be different, but there are plenty of ways you can ensure that it doesn't feel like a change for the worse.

So, as you're reading this book, I'm going to presume that you're going to be a dad, you're perhaps thinking about fatherhood, that you are a pregnant woman looking to find a helpful book for your partner, or you're someone with a man in your life who is about to experience fatherhood for the first time. Well, whatever the reason you're reading this book, you've made a sensible choice that will help you (or the man you're thinking of) cope with this momentous change. However this book made its way into your hands, you are very welcome, and I know you'll find it helpful.

Fatherhood can be a scary idea. You might be panicking about your ability to be a dad. How're you going to know what to do? How will you make sure you're being as helpful as possible to your partner without feeling like your life has disappeared forever? How are you going to make sure that your child is safe, loved, and has the best start in life? Well, this book is a great first step in addressing some of those problems.

In this book, I'm going to take you through the main changes you can expect as a result of fatherhood, as well as giving you techniques and skills that will help you cope with these, both in terms of practical problem solving and emotional support. 'Hero Dad Mindset' is not a patronising explanation of how your partner might not want as much sex as before, or how you need to help out by cooking dinner every now and again—I'm going to speak to you as an adult. Changes are afoot, that much is certain. This book will help you prepare for these changes, so that you can feel calm, helpful, and part of an effective partnership with the mother of your child.

So, why should you listen to me? Firstly, I'm a qualified psychologist with over 17 years of experience of working with adult men who have struggled with a number of problems in their lives, one of which has often been coping with the changes in their lives that have come as a result of becoming a dad. I'm also a father myself, to a seven-year-old girl and a ten month old boy, so I can attest to the usefulness of the techniques and information included in this book. I've test driven them myself, and I've have found them to be useful and invaluable.

Having worked with adult men over many years, I've seen first-hand the improvement in their lives as a result of the material in this book. They have experienced improvements in their lives in many ways, such as in the terms of their experiences of fatherhood, their relationship with the mother of their children, and a strengthening of their bonds with their children. This book has been a central part of this process of improving their lives in general, and it has supported their ability to find fatherhood a blissful and very enjoyable part of their lives.

I promise that if you read through this book, you'll be much better informed about the changes that are to come, as well as being much better equipped to manage these changes in a calm and productive way. You will be more relaxed and content, and able to manage most challenges that fatherhood can bring. You will also be much more likely to find even the trickiest parts of fatherhood enjoyable. The book is a concise, clearly written, and easy-to-understand guide to managing the changes that come with fatherhood in a stress free and psychologically informed way.

If you feel like fatherhood is a terrifying prospect, or if you worry that you're not going to be able to make the changes in your life without feeling resentful or anxious, then this is the book for you. Or, if you are the partner of someone who is about to become a father, or are thinking about starting a family with a man who may have concerns about fatherhood, then getting this book in front of them is probably one of the most helpful things you can do.

So, what are you waiting for?

HOW TO USE THIS BOOK

Congratulations! If you've made it this far, you're already one step closer to experiencing fatherhood in a less stressful and challenging way. It may be that you bought this book for yourself, being somewhat aware of some of the challenges ahead. Or, the book may have made its way to you through the hands of another person who thinks it may benefit you (most likely your partner if you're planning to start a family, or the mother of your child if there is already a baby on the scene). It might be that you are already a father. That is not a problem, and I'm confident that this book can still be of great benefit to you.

However this book got to you, I'm glad it has. I'm also confident about how you will feel once you have had time to read and digest the contents. So, I'm expecting that you are interested about what you can expect to find in this book. The book has four main parts, and the contents of these different parts are outlined below.

After these initial introductory chapters, you will find part one of this book. Part one is focused on assessing your readiness for fatherhood. This section is particularly helpful if you are someone who is mulling over the idea of becoming a father. It might be that the issue of children has cropped up in your current relationship, and that you are at a point where you're thinking about taking this important step. Don't panic if you're already in a position where you're going to become a father, this section can still be useful. Learning that you are due to become a father can panic the most calm man, so there is a chapter here about getting your head around the news and starting to come to terms with the big change on the horizon. Also, part one of this book spends some time considering what your hopes and fears for fatherhood are, before exploring some of the myths and expectations about pregnancy and fatherhood that can be problematic and unhelpful.

Part two of this book is about a paradigm shift. This sounds very grand, but it's basically a way of explaining that, when the child arrives, your life will change. This is going to lead to some difficult changes and stresses in your life, which are going to be novel, and they're going to test your relationship, despite how strong you think it currently is. This part of the book therefore is particularly useful in terms of helping you as a father begin to make peace with the changes that are coming.

It is not uncommon to feel concerned about how your life will change—this doesn't make you a bad person or an unloving or uncommitted father. I have found myself explaining to numerous impending fathers that they need to prepare themselves for quadrupling how hard they predict parenting can be at times. I thought I was ready, and in many ways I was. However, there were plenty of things that took me by surprise and really stretched my coping and resilience as a person and as a partner.

Part three of the book moves matters on to life after the birth of your child. This part of the book begins by exploring the impact of the day of the arrival of your little one. The day can be joyous and exciting, but there are also parts which can be stressful and anxiety provoking. What is your role as father, and what can you do to help your partner? The book then moves on to consider ways that you can ensure that the channels of communication remain open and functional between you and the mother of your child, as well as some of the main ways that you can offer support to both your partner and your child, and this support can be practical or emotional in nature.

This third section of the book also outlines some of the ways in which you can remain on top of your own emotional management, so that you are contributing to a calm and relaxed environment for your family, and so that you are not experiencing negative emotions that might leak out in unhelpful ways. There are also many practical suggestions about how you can manage your time.

Depending on your lifestyle, you may already feel that you don't have enough hours in the day to do all of the things that you want and like to do. Well, those hours are now going to be squeezed even more, and sacrifices need to be made. That does not mean giving up your identity totally, though, and this is where this part of the book can be a great help. One of the chapters in this part of the book talks about teamwork with the mother of your child. This teamwork can be achieved, regardless of the status of your relationship with the mother of your child. You may be in a cohabiting relationship, you may not have ever been in a relationship, or you may no longer be in a relationship with this person. Whatever the status of your relationship, teamwork is pivotal to being an effective father.

The final part of the book moves on to look at what happens after the initial early years of your child's life. What are the longer term considerations you need to make to ensure you are being the best father you can be? There are crucial things to bear I mind, such as the example you are setting as a father, and your developing relationship and bond with your child. Finally, there is a summary of immediate next steps you might be able to take to ensure you are well on your way to making the most out of fatherhood and maximising the chances of finding it a positive experience and one that is as calm and relaxing as possible.

So, that is what you can expect from this book. It is designed to be a guidebook to help you navigate some of the tricky parts of fatherhood and parenting more generally. Fatherhood can be stressful at times, and this book is focused on striving to help you avoid undue stress, anxiety, and resentment, and to do all of this in a psychologically safe way. The chapters are labelled in clear and concise ways in an effort to make it easy for you to select bits you want to concentrate on. I, of course, suggest that you read it all from front to back, but I would say that. You are, of course, welcome to just read the bits you think apply directly to you, or that you think you will benefit from the most. However you choose to use this book, I am very confident that you will take a number of useful things away from your experience of reading it.

I also need to explain what this book is not. There are plenty of books about fatherhood already, so what makes this one different? Well, this book is not a patronising rundown of what a nappy is, or why your partner might be suddenly a bit grumpy. I'm sorry if you wanted some of that nuts and bolts advice, but you won't find much of that here. Instead, you will have a set of things you can do to help prepare psychologically for fatherhood to cope with some of the challenges and stresses that people do not spend as much time talking about when it comes to becoming a father.

For whatever reason you're reading this book, or how you plan to read it, it's great to have you here.

PART ONE
GET READY

ONE
ARE YOU READY?

Fatherhood is a big step. That's quite an understatement, but it's worth thinking about what changes are likely to be ahead as a result of this change and what you might need to be considering and expecting as part of this change. We don't always think about all of the alterations that fatherhood will lead to in our lives, and sometimes we don't realise them until it's too late.

The goal of this chapter is get you to start thinking about some of the changes you may need to make and to work out whether you're approaching psychological readiness for fatherhood. Being a father is much more than changing nappies and doing your fair share of feeding (although they are part of it). It is a process of active involvement that you are signing up to, basically for ever. I'm not trying to be melodramatic, but I am trying to make the point that if fatherhood is on the horizon, so should change be. If you think that your life will not change, you're probably being naïve or wilfully unrealistic about your role in the child's life.

So, how do you know if you're ready?

This chapter is not designed to panic you. It might be the case that you actually are ready for fatherhood, but this might not be immediately obvious to you. Like other skills and roles in life, some men will take to this role like a duck to water. You are likely to feel a tinge of fear and anxiety about fatherhood (hopefully alongside feelings such as excitement and hope); let me be among the first to reassure you that these feelings of trepidation are normal. I'd be more worried if you experienced none of these feelings about the impending responsibility ahead.

Thinking about fatherhood probably conjures images of nappies, helping to provide for a family (instead of perhaps just yourself and a partner), wrestling with car seats, school clothes, cars, weddings, education, and tuition—the list is endless! On top of this, there is all the developmental stuff, being a good role model, being responsible, and being a nurturer and a teacher, as well as a confidant and friend—it's a big and varied role!

Surely any sane man would just walk away from this level of stress and responsibility?

Well, the truth is, fatherhood is all of the above. But it is also a truckload of good things too. It can be fun, exciting, enjoyable, incredibly rewarding, and one of the most satisfying and fulfilling roles a man can have.

Below are some key questions. If you don't feel positive about your answers, it might be that now is not the right time for you to think about fatherhood (if that choice is still within your control). If you don't feel good about your answers and still want to be a father, or your child is already on the way, it's time to get yourself sorted and start to initiate some changes in your life; otherwise, fatherhood is going to feel like an unwelcome sledgehammer. If you do feel good about your answers, then you can feel a little more confident that the time is right for you.

Can you de-prioritise yourself and your current goals without experiencing excessive resentment?

Being a father means making sacrifices. Some of these are practical—some activities away from home might need to be reduced for a few years. It might be that you can't spend all that money you've been quietly saving on yourself—it's needed for a cot and a car seat.

These are the kinds of questions you need to be asking yourself. This might seem like an easy question now, but fast forward a year. You've not been out with friends for a while, can't remember the last time you watched your favourite TV show, or had an hour of uninterrupted time on your games console, and you've spent three hours trying to soothe your child to sleep—can you do that without being incredibly resentful and frustrated? I'm not suggesting your life is over with fatherhood, but you do need to adopt a more flexible approach to your personal needs then you have needed to before, and this can be a difficult adjustment for some men. The most successful fathers can balance their own needs with those of their family though, so it is possible.

Do you have a meaningful support network?

Fatherhood can be scary and stressful. It can be made easier by having supportive and helpful people around you, outside of you and your partner. Are your extended families supportive of you having a child? What about your friends? If you're working, what are your employers like when it comes to family life? To a degree, they are legally obliged to fulfil certain commitments, but some jobs better match parenting than others—not that this alone should make or break your choice of course.

Have you got people you could turn to in a moment of crisis? People who are there for you to talk to, express frustration to, and just spend time with can be enormously helpful. My wife and I are very lucky to have a supportive family. I'll always remember my wife saying that my own father was a great support when I returned to work after paternity leave. She could just take our daughter up to his house, walk through the front door, and he would take my daughter from my wife, while she sat and had probably her first cup of tea that day! That kind of support is invaluable.

Are you and your partner a team?

You might be living with the mother of your child, or not. Either way, fatherhood is much easier if you consider the mother of your child as your teammate. That means that this relationship needs to be functional and safe, as this is the bedrock of successful co-parenting. You might need to invest some time in ensuring this relationship functions well—this is the person who will help you get more sleep and ensure that you retain as much sanity as possible. I recall my wife and I taking fifteen-minute shifts trying to comfort our daughter when she had colic one night. That that was just enough time to cool down and recharge, ready to relieve the other person. You have to be prepared to be absolutely fair in the choices you make. It's a good habit to get into early on, and the added benefit is that, when your child is older, they learn great lessons about positive relationships and parenting.

Do you have, or can you find positive role models?

Not all men are lucky enough to have great fathers to learn from. But, just because you may not have had the best father, doesn't mean there is any reason why you cannot be a great father yourself. I'm constantly amazed how often I hear my own father's voice coming out of my own mouth—I guess that's the power of conditioning! You might have a great friend who is a good father, or an uncle, or a cousin—anyone in fact. If there is a man you know who was/is a great father you want to emulate, get in touch and bend their ear. If they deserve your respect then you know they're bound to listen and help you.

Have you actually thought about parenting?

This might sound obvious, but I'm talking about an active process of consideration here. Have you weighed up the pros and cons of parenting? Have you started to think about things you may need to give up or change in your life (at least in the short term), or is your head in the sand and you keep finding yourself saying things like "I'm sure it will be fine," or "How hard can it be anyway?"

Invest time in talking these issues through with your partner and actually do some thinking! What do you want for your children? What do you want to teach them, and how do you want them to view you? Most of us want our children to think nice things about us, but the love and respect of our children is not an entitlement. We have to earn it, and that takes work. Are you ready to do that work?

Are you mature and mostly sensible in other areas of your life?

I'm not asking if you are a soulless robot who doesn't know how to have a good time. I'm asking if you know how to budget money? Do you tend to do the right things (even when no-one is looking), and do you have positive core values that you can pass on to a child? Are you someone who takes responsibility and has the resilience to dig in and 'do the hard yards' when things get tricky, or do you tend to walk away and avoid difficulty?

Successful fathers tend to be mature and focused on the long term in order to do what's right for the people who depend on them. If you don't feel able to answer this question, ask people you know and trust, and who will answer honestly, even if it hurts your feelings or bruises your ego. This is not the time for undeserved flattery. Also, think about how good you are at managing your temper. If this is a problem for you, it might be best to try to improve your emotional management skills before fatherhood starts. Children can test the most patient people, and tempers can be easily triggered.

Can you cope with the idea that you will need to learn as you go?

Most fathers feel some degree of panic and anxiety when their child arrives. Some people like to know everything about a topic before starting, but that just isn't possible with fatherhood. There are so many individual differences that mean you will never know it all. You need to be okay with this.

So much of good parenting is about trial and error, and getting to know your own child and what does and does not work for them. Books and other people's experiences can be excellent and often spot on, but at other times you need to be prepared to muddle through and figure things out for yourself. Being a good father is not about knowing everything from the start. We all start at zero.

In summary, fatherhood is exciting and an incredible journey. However, it is a journey you need to feel ready for, and one that you are 'agreeing' to sign up for. If this is not the case, fatherhood might feel more difficult than it might otherwise, and, therefore, the above questions are a good place to start to help you think about whether you're ready to take this step in your life.

TWO
COMING TO TERMS WITH UNEXPECTED FATHERHOOD

Learning that you're going to become a father can be a ground-shaking moment. If it's something that has been planned and worked towards, then this moment can be full of excitement and joy. However, if the pregnancy is a surprise or not something you expected or wanted at this point in your life, it can feel very different. This chapter will focus on what to do if you find yourself hearing the news about a pregnancy that you were not expecting.

This is clearly an important issue. If you weren't planning or hoping to become a father in the near future, and then you hear the news that you are going to be a father, your reality is likely to be shaken. You don't need to panic, although it would not be surprising if this was one of the first feelings you experienced.

You need to come to terms with your new potential reality as a father, and whilst achieving this instantaneously is unlikely to be possible, it is not a process that can be dragged out forever. Engaging in this process of making peace with (and dare I say, looking forward to) fatherhood, needs to begin as soon as possible. Not doing this could be psychologically damaging, and it is important to look after your emotional wellbeing.

What Not to Do

- React Quickly and Focus on Yourself

You could have experienced a whole range of strong emotions on hearing the news that you're going to become a father. The important thing to do is not react to feelings of panic and say or do something which you could later come to regret. It might be that the news is a bolt from the blue, a total surprise that you never expected in your wildest dreams. Remember that the woman involved is also feeling the same way, so try your best to think about how she is also likely to be feeling. Words can hurt, especially if she is feeling anxious about breaking the news to you—that could have taken a huge amount of courage to do.

- Rush into Decisions

After the news has landed will come the realisation that whatever path you take, life will feel different. It is really important that choices you make at this point feel well thought out, and they are made compassionately and sensitively, having gone through a careful process of considering the options. Give yourself some time to process the news, but be really clear with the woman involved that you are not ignoring the situation, and agree to a time to catch up and discuss the issue. This will help her to know you are processing rather than ignoring, and it also gives you some space to process your thoughts and feelings properly.

- Run Away

You are unlikely to be the only person concerned or worried about unexpected fatherhood. Stay in contact with the woman (if she is not a long term partner) and keep her informed about how you are thinking and feeling about the situation and how you would like to be involved in decision making and the pregnancy more generally. Don't leave room for misunderstanding or assumption; communicate regularly and clearly, and, of course, always respectfully.

What to Do

- Listen

A surprise pregnancy is difficult for men and women. Your initial role might just be to listen to how your partner feels about the situation. You can obviously share your thoughts too, but don't underestimate the importance of just listening with compassion. Ask questions about how she is feeling and what changes she notices. This will help to improve your understanding of her perspective and also help her to feel supported and considered. Any decisions that then get reached will feel more collaborative and shared, as opposed to one party feeling coerced or forced into a choice they are not comfortable with.

- Talk to Someone you Trust

You can talk to the woman who is pregnant, of course, but you may want to talk to someone who is objective. Perhaps there is someone in your life who also experienced an unexpected pregnancy—they can often share experiences in a useful way that will help you to feel better informed. Make sure it is someone you trust, as you need to feel able to be really honest with how you think and feel about the situation without the fear of being judged.

- Be Honest

Now is not the time to say what you think is right, or whatever you think other people want you to say. Be true to yourself and express your fears. This allows the person involved to share their fears too, and you can reassure each other and discuss how these fears and concerns could be addressed.

- Fake it 'Till You Make It

This sounds contrary to the above point, but it isn't. The above point is more about your communication with others. This point is more about your internal monologue and thinking style. It might be that you've always wanted to be a father, but that this has arrived earlier in your life than you expected. Try focusing exclusively on the benefits of fatherhood. Over time, these may become more and more important and believable to you. It might be that it's not long before this internal reinforcement has helped you to come to terms with the situation, and you can actually start to look forward to it in a more natural and genuine way.

In summary, a surprise pregnancy can be tricky for all

the people involved. As the father to be, people will look to you quite quickly to start to fill a role you may not feel you are anywhere near ready for. The process of making sense of the impending change in your life can take time, and this is normal. Be kind to yourself and allow this process to happen. Don't shut out the pregnant woman involved, even if all you can tell her is that you are still actively thinking and working through your thoughts, at least she will know that you are being proactive, rather than avoidant about the situation. In a way, this process is good practice for the open and meaningful communication that is going to be so valuable moving forward as you experience joint parenting.

THREE
FATHERHOOD FEARS

This chapter is going to explore and consider some of the main fears and concerns that men can have about fatherhood. It is worth considering some of the common fears in detail, as they can be wrapped up in myths, and myth-busting is one of the most effective ways of helping to manage fears about fatherhood.

Not all men will have the same fears about fatherhood. Some men will have very individual fears that are personal to them, and these can span any number of different topics. With this in mind, as well as some myth-busting, this chapter will also help to explain a method that you can use independently (alone or with another person) to help you explore your fears in detail and make an objective assessment about how valid and useful they actually are.

So, below are some common fears that men have about becoming a father, along with some helpful information that will, hopefully, help you to feel a bit more relaxed about the key issues:

- I'm going to be useless and helpless at the birth

There has recently been an explosion of reality television series which depict real birth. I think this has been useful as a way of shedding light on some of the process, but it can heighten anxieties when things go wrong or take an unexpected turn. The bit fathers are *responsible* for is reassuring the mother and being supportive throughout the process—luckily, that's something that requires no formal training or qualifications. The medical staff are the skilled ones, and they need to make the decisions; your role as father is to be there and concentrate on the mother.

Try to find ways to be as involved as possible, which should help you feel a bit more in control. Become familiar with the mother's birthing plan. You should know the plan as well as she does, and there's no reason you can't be very aware of its contents. Your midwife may have some good ideas too about how you can get more involved. The word *your* in the last sentence was not accidental; the midwife is a source of comfort and information for both of you. Ultimately, at the birth, your main role is to be a calming and supportive presence at the delivery. Reassure and comfort your partner. This is likely to be the most helpful contribution you can make during your child's birth.

- I'm not ready to be a dad

This is a biggy, and it's probably one of the most significant concerns that an impending father might have. Some people might worry that becoming a father means the end of their own youth, or that they now need to sacrifice everything they enjoy doing in life. The idea of growing up and being a proper adult can be quite daunting, but it's important to remember that millions of men have gone through the process and made the change very successfully.

Another thing to bear in mind is that becoming a father helps you to see life in a whole new way. Enjoyable experiences are heightened and, over time, some things naturally become less important to you as your family grows. You also get to do the stuff you always liked; you just may need to get better at planning and negotiation. You may become more mature, but this is not the same as becoming old. The two processes are different! I have to say in many ways I felt like fatherhood gave me a new lease of life. Despite the extra physical tiredness, I felt incredibly positive about life and the future.

- I don't know how to look after a baby and won't be able to do it

This is quite a common concern, and one that is quite understandable. Parenting and caring for another human in terms of quite basic needs is a skill and one that needs to be developed over time. Most people want to succeed at the things they do, and this is also likely to be true of caring for our children. Men might feel particularly concerned about this because, in many ways, their childhoods may not have included much leaning towards caring for others, and the societal stereotype that women 'are just better' at this is unlikely to be helping. Television doesn't help. In dramas and sitcoms, fathers are often portrayed as extra children—caring and loving, but generally hapless buffoons, especially when it comes to looking after babies and children.

It might be worth trying to get a bit of exposure to babies

who you may already have close to you. This can help you to feel a bit less scared about caring for one yourself. There are also plenty of excellent books about childcare for men that cover topics such as emotional management and effective and appropriate discipline. The reality of the situation is that the basics of childcare are relatively straightforward and, like all skills, expertise comes with everyday practice. It's not just the child who should not be expected to run before they can walk!

- My relationship with my partner will change and I won't like it

Guess what? Your relationship will change. But that's not necessarily a bad thing. After our daughter was born I felt much closer to my wife. We had created something amazing together and, even when it was really challenging and difficult, I felt like we were much more of a team than we had been at points before she was born.

One of the things that can be a tricky adjustment is no longer being the sole focus of your partner's attention. It may sound extreme, but some men can feel neglected and jealous after the arrival of a child, and if not managed correctly, this can lead to resentment and problems.

You can try to reduce the impact of the changes in your relationship by planning a specific time for you and your partner to spend time together. When your child is a little older, you might arrange babysitters and have 'date nights' together, but don't be surprised if those initial ones are spent talking about your child or worrying about them! In the early days even snatching a few hours together to have a short walk or watch a film can be really important and give you a chance to talk and continue to feel connected. My wife and I found this to be really helpful in the early days.

- I can't afford a child; there isn't enough money!

Another common concern about impending fatherhood is finances. There's no escaping the fact that children are expensive, so if it was a purely financial decision, I think most people would choose not to have children. Kids come with a lot of stuff, such as prams, cots, and nappies, and it all adds up, and this can put a strain on family finances (potentially complicated by one of you no longer working and being on maternity pay). The truth of the matter is that no one saves up £200,000 and then decides to have a child. Life isn't like that, so you need to make the best of what you've got and stretch your money as far as possible.

If you're not great at budgeting, there's no better reason than having a child on the way to get better at it! Hopefully, you have around nine months to get your financial house in order as much as possible, so take advantage of that time to start forming good and healthy financial habits. Try not to worry about branded products and the latest posy buggy—children don't care what the writing on the side of their pram is as long as they are fed, warm, and loved. Just get what you need and make sure it's safe and functional.

There are likely to be monthly expenditures that can be cut down or removed. Remember, this is not necessarily forever. It might just be that you don't need more than one television streaming service for the next few years. Things that are cut can always return when things are a bit more settled. Thinking about it in these terms can help, as short term sacrifices are easier to accept than permanent ones.

- Other fears and concerns

There will be plenty of other quite individual and specific concerns that expectant fathers might have, and I would never be able to capture them all here. Therefore, below is a series of steps to go through with your concern/fear. Following this process should allow you to accurately assess how relevant your fear is, and often this in itself can help to address some of your negative emotions:

1. Maintain an open mind. Recognise that you might not need to be as fearful and maybe don't need to be fearful at all. People can be overconfident in the validity and accuracy of their views. Ask yourself if you are certain you are right, and consider other times in your life when the reality of a situation was not as bad as your fears about it.

2. Get some distance from the fears. Get some distance from your emotions so you can objectively assess your fears. Try some mindfulness and meditation/relaxation, or get your energy levels up; these can be great ways of relieving the pressure of strong emotions.

3. Examine the evidence from a broad perspective. Conduct some research on the prevalence in the broader population of the issues underlying your fears. Use reputable, objective sources and not ones that will simply confirm your fears. Based on what you learn, how do the issues underlying your fears stack up against the data on the prevalence of those issues?

4. Examine the evidence from a narrow perspective. How widespread are the issues in your own community? Your community might differ markedly from the general population. How do the issues measure up against the data in your community? Talk to people with relevant experience you know well and trust—can they provide some counter evidence for your fear/concern?

5. Examine recent exposures to events and information that could create biases that support your fears. Has anything happened in your family, friends' families, or community related to your fears? Have you heard a lot recently in the news about incidents related to the issues underlying your fears? Have you been watching films or television focused on your fears? If you answered yes to any of those questions, consider whether that exposure reflects reality in terms of the prevalence of the issues underlying your fears. Realise that you could suffer from the availability bias in which people rely on recent exposure to specific events and information to form their opinions even when those events and information are out of the norm. Objective data can be really helpful here.

In summary, the knowledge that you are about to become a

father can be concerning, and there can be some very specific concerns, some or all of which may be explored above. Whatever your personal fears and concerns are, it is important that you seek to address them, either through educating yourself where there may be gaps in your knowledge, challenging your own thinking with the above steps, or probably most usefully, talking to others you trust who have been through the experience. Fatherhood will always be a bit scary, that's probably unavoidable. It doesn't need to be terrifying and paralysing though.

FOUR
EXPECTATION VS REALITY

Parenthood is an experience that is difficult to fully appreciate until you actually go through it yourself. I know this can be true of many very different types of experiences, but parenthood is all around us all the time, in our families and in society more widely. Therefore, we tend to end up with a whole set of beliefs about parenthood (both positive and negative), almost whether we wanted to have an opinion about these things or not!

These beliefs are fine in themselves, but the difficulty can be that they start to reinforce expectations about parenthood, which may be helpful, or actually quite unhelpful, when we come to experience parenthood ourselves. If you hold and value pre-determined expectations of fatherhood, then it is potentially going to be problematic if these turn out not to be quite true in your case. All fathers and children are different, so our pre-conceived expectations can be way off the reality of the situation.

This is why we need to spend some time considering the potential reality of fatherhood expectations:

. . .

Expectation: My children will be so well disciplined they will never show me up in public

Reality – Yes they will! I can assure you that no amount of reading about the topic or consistent parenting will ever stop children from having tantrums and misbehaving at some point. The best thing to do is accept that we all have off days, and your child will too. They will be completely irrational at times, and tricks and strategies that have worked hundreds of times before will inexplicably suddenly not work.

The most embarrassing incident I've had with my daughter so far is subjecting her to a fireman's lift and leaving a party, because she outright refused point blank to thank the girl who had invited her to the party. She is generally very polite and motivated to be so, but on this day she just refused. We responded by telling her she would not be allowed a party bag if she did not thank the birthday girl for her invitation, which led to the meltdown and our slightly unorthodox exit.

The good news is that most other people will have been involved in managing this scenario too at one point or another. They will understand what you are going through and are likely to be surprisingly tolerant. I remember noticing a few knowing smiles and sympathetic nods, as I left that party with a red face and a screaming child.

The reality is that all children misbehave at times, so don't set yourself up to fail by expecting perfect behaviour. Disciplining children is one of the most challenging aspects of parenthood, and it takes a huge amount of patience to work out the best way of helping our children understand why what they have done is wrong.

Expectation: All these other parents are rubbish at time management – I'll be able to do all the things I can do now

Reality – You probably won't be able to carry on exactly as you were before, and there are likely to be sacrifices you will need to make. Parenting is a full-time job that eats up time in a way that you may not have experienced before. Even if you're a multi-tasking prioritising machine, things crop up all the time that you just cannot plan for. Your child will be sick at the most inconvenient times. You will be needed at home to assist with any number of unplanned emergencies. One of the things I learned early on after becoming a father was that I needed to change my language. Instead of 'I'm going for a run later,' it became 'I hope to go for a run later.' It just makes the disappointment easier to accept if your plans need to change at short notice.

Expectation – I will have a perfect work life balance and never feel worried that I am neglecting my child or my career

Reality – Since my daughter arrived, I have spent my whole life feeling guilty/anxious that I am neglecting one of these things. It is difficult to avoid these feelings I think, unless you decide to be a parent who doesn't work. Even then it is not guaranteed that you will avoid guilt. I've been in some really tricky situations where I felt like I had to choose, and that can be really unpleasant. Ultimately, I settled on a position where I just wanted to feel that my daughter would feel I had time for her and that she never played second fiddle to my career. It can be a challenge though, so prepare for some tough choices. I think the goal is probably to strive for a feeling of meaningful connection with your child, so even if you are not physically with them as much as you would be in an ideal world, the time you do have together is high quality and significant.

Expectation: Once my child is asleep I will get a full night's sleep and can concentrate on all the things I want to do without any interruption

Reality – Parenting is one of those jobs that doesn't stop. There is no 'clocking off' as such, and even when your child is soundly asleep, you are likely to still (certainly initially) tend to worry about them. You can find yourself worrying if they are too hot or too cold, or waiting for them to wake up and disturb whatever you've been looking forward to for a big part of the day..

I remember the frustration of being alone with my daughter for the night while my wife had a rare evening out. I had chosen my favourite film to watch and the long awaited Chinese takeaway had just arrived. That was exactly the point in time my daughter woke up and took over an hour to settle back to sleep. By that point the takeaway was cold, and I was very grumpy—it can be very stressful!

. . .

Expectation – I need to have lots of money before I can consider becoming a parent

Reality – Raising a child is a very expensive business. The reality is, very few people save up the thousands of pounds children cost before having them. The population would not be sustainable if this approach was taken! Many people have children and look after them very successfully without being wealthy. You do need to budget, and make sensible choices about money, but this is something that can be planned for a lot of the time, or, if not, at least in the months before the arrival you can start to make changes to your less helpful financial habits. If you haven't shared your finances with a partner before, you may need to get used to being quite transparent about them. If one parent feels that the other is being a bit sneaky or dishonest about their financial situation, it doesn't take much for resentment to spill over into conflict. All of this is avoidable with honesty.

Expectation – My child will excel in everything they do, always make the right choices, and do everything I want them to do

Reality – Your child will be a human and probably not a genius or a superstar. That doesn't mean they cannot achieve your respect, admiration, and pride. They will make some good choices and some bad ones, just like you did. The key is not to be unrealistic about your expectations for your child. Ensuring that you teach them resilience, and to always try their best at whatever they're doing, means you are likely to end up with a hard working child with a pragmatic and realistic sense of what they want to achieve, and how they should behave in life.

If your child feels pressure to achieve unrealistic goals that you have set for them, they might end up feeling terrified of disappointing you and conversely less likely to succeed in the way you would like. Also, they may be more susceptible to lower self-esteem and negative thinking about themselves.

Instead of having unrealistic expectations, think about how you can help your children understand what might be realistic goals for them as they develop, and this skill is one they can carry forward into adulthood. Realistic goals can, of course, be ambitious, which is also a great thing to instil in a child, but they need to be reachable. Children need to feel stretched, but not so much that they miss their target and experience unpleasant consequences because of that. Positive reinforcement will encourage further good efforts, and helping children 'bounce back' from setbacks and disappointment will encourage resilience.

Expectations – We will have amazing family holidays in incredible exotic locations

Reality – Children come with a lot of stuff. Travelling anywhere with children, especially in the first year or so, even to the local ships can be quite complex. They have a lot of immediate needs that you need to be able to respond to right away and often this means that you will need the correct tools and equipment in order to do this. Also, as children get older, you are more likely to find yourself in Peppa Pig World than Mauritius. The good news is that one of the most enjoyable things about parenting is seeing your child happy, and listening out for squeals of excitement is also good fun.

Holidays, therefore, are likely to be more difficult to achieve. This is not the same as saying it is impossible, though, as it is not. And, as with most things to do with children, more planning beforehand can make them perfectly doable. For the short term, spontaneity is something that will be less prevalent in your life.

In summary, there are a number of beliefs and expectations that can arise before you actually experience being a parent. The reality can often be quite different. This does not have to be a source of disappointment or stress, though. You just need to remember to be kind to yourself and realistic about what you expect from yourself, your partner, and your child. Life won't be the same after you've become a father, but that doesn't mean it has to be worse. You just need to be prepared for it to be different.

FIVE
PLANNING TO HAVE A CHILD

So far in this book we've looked at some of the fears around fatherhood, some of the expectations you might have, and how these actually stack up against reality. This chapter will focus on the process of planning to have a child. Therefore, if your partner is already pregnant and the child is on their way, you can probably skip this chapter. However, if you and your partner have decided that now is the time to start working towards conceiving, this chapter is likely to be important.

This chapter is important for a few reasons. Firstly, there is quite a lot to think about in terms of trying to conceive. I think most men will tend to presume that it will be plain sailing, that it is just a matter of time before your partner becomes pregnant, and that there is going to be lots of sex in the meantime.

This is true in some cases, but not so in others. Fertility is complex, and sometimes conceiving can take longer than you might expect, which can be stressful in itself. This chapter explores key issues relating to the process of planning to have a child and conceiving, and how to manage your own (as well as your partner's) emotional and psychological wellbeing during this process. Here are some questions to ask yourself and perhaps discuss with your partner:

Who should we tell we are trying?

This depends very much on the type of people you are. Some people like to share all of their lives (especially with the advent of social media). Others are more private. Think carefully about who you want to share this intensely personal journey with. It is probably wise to have at least one confidant you can talk to (apart from your partner) but you might not want to cast the net too wide.

If things get difficult and your partner struggles to conceive, well-meaning questions and requests for updates from friends and family can feel like hammer blows. Love and support from friends and family helps, but they are not all equally skilled at judging what to say and what to avoid saying. My wife doesn't enjoy being the centre of attention, so we decided to keep our plans to ourselves. You will know your inner circle well, and it's important to reach an agreement with your partner about who you will share the information with (if anyone at all).

How long does it take to conceive?

This is a very difficult question to give a definitive answer to.

It's a process you and your partner have very limited control over, so it's worth preparing emotionally for a process that can feel completely random. It could happen very quickly, or it could take a long time.

If it does take longer than you anticipated, it can be difficult to cope with pregnancies that are starting for people you know, and I guarantee you will never see more pregnant people day to day than you will when you're trying to conceive. There is something about the way the brain works (as well as availability bias) that will make you think there is suddenly a huge increase in rates of pregnancy in your local area. There probably isn't, and it's much more likely to be your brain picking up on something that is now much more relevant to you than it previously was.

By way of rough estimation, the experts recommend that healthy couples who want to conceive try for a year if they're younger than 35, and six months if they're 35 or older. Talk with your doctor if it doesn't happen by then. These discussions with medical experts can feel daunting, and you (or your partner) could end up feeling different or that you're broken.

All I can say is that I've really had my eyes opened to the levels of difficulty that people experience with conception. If you do experience difficulties, you're one of many, not one of the few, as I previously thought. My and my wife's journey to conception was not straightforward, and we needed medical intervention, which was ultimately successful. The chances that it is impossible for you to conceive at all are slim, so enter these conversations with medical experts with an open mind and a positive mind frame.

. . .

How do I manage the pressure to perform?

When you're trying to conceive, the fact of the matter is that sex can become difficult. This might sound hard to believe, especially if you and your partner are particularly sexually active. However, whereas sex for the sake of it is mostly fun and enjoyable, sex 'with a mission' (i.e. to conceive) can feel different. You might find yourself being asked to perform on demand, and that your sex life now adheres to a strict timetable which involves less spontaneity and romance, with a slight shift towards function and results. Your partner might be undergoing some fairly intrusive procedures during this time, and that can add to any sense of pressure you may be feeling, as you might have an awareness that as soon as pregnancy occurs, some of these procedures can stop.

This shift in approach to sex (and it will not be the case for all couples trying to conceive) can be difficult to cope with psychologically. If you're not careful, you may end up feeling that you have been reduced to a sperm donor. This is why, if there's a sudden shift in your sex life in an effort to conceive, that you do not lose the more emotional connection you have with your partner.

Don't forget to keep talking, and don't view sex as an activity that is purely about conception; it's also about expressing love and affection for your partner. If you do find yourself becoming preoccupied with conception and this is adding pressure, you could come to an arrangement where your partner doesn't tell you when she is ovulating, so that certain occasions when you have sex are not standing out in your mind as more important in terms of you 'succeeding' in delivering semen.

. . .

Should we avoid baby focused activities?

The human brain is fantastic at putting the things that are in our subconscious right at the centre of our attention. That means that even if you're trying not to obsess about pregnancy, you will see more pregnant people then you've ever seen in your life. If your own journey to conception is proving difficult, this can really add unwanted stress and negative emotions into the mix, for both you and your partner.

Therefore, you may decide that whilst you are trying to conceive that you avoid babies and related topics. Obviously, to a degree, contact with babies and children is unavoidable, but if you are in the midst of a difficult and stressful process towards conception, it's probably wise not to go to christenings and baby showers that you don't need to. If you won't be missed and going to such an event would cause you significant stress, why expose yourself to that? It's not raining on anyone's parade to simply take yourself (or for your partner to do the same) out of the equation—that's much better than spending hours dealing with the emotional fallout afterwards.

If you find yourself in the company of someone who is casually talking about how easily they conceived, it's okay and quite normal to feel envy and some irritation. Try not to say anything out loud though. Perhaps you could write it down later and then destroy it. That could help to dissipate some of the main negative emotion.

If it's a close friend or someone you see regularly, perhaps consider letting them know about your own conception journey. This can be difficult, but it will help them understand why you might seem a little more distant, or at least not particularly motivated to engage in lots of pregnancy and baby focused chat for a while. If they really are your friend, they will understand your difficult position and respect your needs.

Finally, never forget that you don't know someone else's story. They might tell everyone it was an accident, but for all you know they've been secretly trying for years. Smile inwardly to yourself in the knowledge that when your time comes, you'll be much more discreet and thoughtful about it.

It was a huge learning curve for me, and since becoming a father, I've never proactively asked anyone else if they've thought about having children. I now know and understand the sensitivities and stresses that could be lurking in private lives.

Should my partner do a pregnancy test early?

This is a really difficult one. This will probably depend on your personality, as well as that of your partner, but, in many ways, it's a waste of time. The temptation to do will be strong, and minds can be clever and cruel enough to play tricks and convince women they are experiencing pregnancy related symptoms, even if they aren't pregnant.

Try to stay grounded if your partner reports these symptoms. It is particularly cruel that pregnancy symptoms are similar to symptoms which suggest a period is on the way. Your job here is to help your partner feel optimistic, but also pragmatically prepare for the news you don't want to hear. I would suggest you try and support your partner in waiting until the time is right in her menstrual cycle. Perhaps use this time to do fun things together that don't involve trying to conceive or talking or thinking about conception.

Ultimately, you'll probably end up deciding to do whatever your partner wants to do (you can't police her toilet use after all—nor should you try)! If your partner can be persuaded to wait, that's probably the wisest way forward. You don't want to end up spending lots of money on expensive pregnancy tests. Talk to your partner about the fact that a negative test is likely to just make them feel sad (and you still won't know for certain), whereas, if she waits for her period to arrive, at least then she'll be on the first day of her next cycle, and you both can start trying again in a few days. Psychologically, it's easier on the soul and less likely to feel quite so stressful.

Should I give up alcohol and smoking too?

There are lots of things your partner can do to prepare for pregnancy and boost the chances of conception. It is widely accepted that activities like smoking and consuming alcohol are not that helpful for pregnancy. Your partner may decide to stop doing these things before she becomes pregnant. You may decide to make some changes to your lifestyle too.

This may seem less necessary, but there are links between healthy sperm and alcohol consumption and smoking, so now is not a bad time to take a look at some of the changes you could make. This has the dual benefit of being very supportive of your partner and improving your own general health (which means that, hopefully, you can run around more with a child one day—they tend to have a crazy amount of energy)! Don't feel like you're never allowed a pint anymore, but at least cutting down is likely to be highly appreciated by your partner.

Why can't my partner pull herself together?

Trying to conceive is an incredibly emotional journey. It can be complicated at times by powerful hormones that some treatments for fertility complications can include, which can have an impact on mood and presentation. It's really important to be as patient as you can with your partner. There will be times this feels really difficult, especially if you are also struggling.

Help your partner process these emotions. Give her your time and attention, and try to spend time together away from your conception goals. There's a reason you're trying to have a child together, so celebrate your relationship. It's realistic to expect tears and periods of low mood. Allow some wallow time—that's part of the process. If it becomes the dominant emotion or presentation though, make sure you are talking to your partner about any extra support you can offer, or if there is any external support she thinks would help.

I have a low sperm count and it's all my fault we can't conceive

. . .

Sperm counts are on the decline generally, for a number of different reasons. I mention this only to highlight that you are not alone, although there is a good chance that this is exactly how you feel. The first thing to remember is that this is unlikely to be a reflection of you or your life choices. Often, these problems are genetic or linked to things that you have little or no control over. Do not despair and do not feel that you are any less of a man than anyone else. Thousands of men are living with reduced or no sperm count, so there is support out there.

Talk to others who can support you. Trusted friends should be able to listen, and there are likely to be support groups (at least on the Internet if not available elsewhere), where you can feel heard and express yourself without fear of judgement. Just as much as you would not 'blame' your partner if she was experiencing complications that made conception difficult, you should not blame yourself if you also experience the same. If you have a reduced, rather than zero sperm count, there are things you can do to help, such as reducing alcohol intake and not smoking. Seek advice about these things, as they could make the difference for you and your partner.

In summary, planning to have a child is an exciting time. The process of trying to conceive can be a lot of fun, but it can also be fraught with stresses and difficulties. If this is the first time you and your partner have ever tried for a child, you don't know yet if it will be straightforward. Fingers crossed it will be, and there is no reason it won't be. But, it might be worth thinking about what you can do if you discover it's not going to be straightforward.

PART TWO
GET SET

SIX
MOTHERHOOD AND SACRIFICE

Pregnancy and childbirth can be a very stressful process, both in terms of the physical impact of growing a person inside their body, as well as the emotional impact of this process. Women experience a huge hormonal shift during pregnancy, and this can take its toll. Women's bodies change during pregnancy, and some of those changes are permanent. It's worth thinking about this more closely. I can't think of any natural processes (outside of ageing) that men experience that have the same impact on our bodies. It is some of these changes that will be covered in this chapter.

So why are we covering this then? I promised at the start of this book that I wasn't going to embark on a patronising lecture about the basis of pregnancy, and I intend to stick to that promise. What this chapter is about is understanding the changes and using this knowledge to help cope with fatherhood.

What's the link you might ask? Well, in some ways, women have a head start in coming to terms with parenting, as they will notice changes to their life much sooner than you will notice changes to yours. Understanding and remembering this helps us men to cope with our own stresses around parenting, and sometimes we just need a little memory jog about the sacrifices of motherhood to help us put our difficulties in perspective, which can help us do our best when we're feeling challenged and under pressure.

Pregnancy is generally a beautiful process to observe, at least from the outside. For the woman experiencing it, it can feel very different, and the symptoms can be painful, embarrassing, and, frankly, quite distressing at times. Aside from the physical changes and aches and pains, there can be a whole host of emotional and psychological consequences that can make this process stressful, and they can have a long lasting impact on the mother of your child. My wife experienced physical discomfort at times, but the things that bothered her the most were the exhaustion and the 'pregnancy brain' (being forgetful and feeling less organised than she normally was were things that she found really difficult to cope with).

Physical changes can be difficult for women to cope with too, especially if they feel they have worked hard to retain a certain figure or body shape. Breasts can sag, stretch marks can appear, and vaginas can change. It's also unlikely that your reassurance that these things are not important will take away all of the bad feelings. I can't imagine going through a process where your body doesn't quite feel the same ever again. This, I'm advised, is the experience of pregnancy and childbirth.

There are also a number of physical symptoms that can lead to discomfort, such as excess gas and bloating, having a less robust pelvic floor that can lead to urine leakage and the odd accident, increased frequency of urination, itching, soreness, constipation, and swelling. This is often all before there is a person inside your partner kicking them all over the place, all in the context of physical exhaustion. One of the symptoms my wife found most distressing was the constant nausea. To top it off, I don't think she actually was sick at any point; she just felt like she was on the brink of vomiting all day. She also experienced gestational diabetes, which was challenging, as she had to learn about testing her sugar levels and inject herself daily.

Psychological changes can also be challenging. Pregnancy and the change in hormones can affect emotional regulation and increase feelings of depression and anxiety. If ever there was a time when it would not be convenient to feel depressed or low, it would be when your body is changing, and you don't feel like your normal self.

So, what was the point of this chapter then? I think as men we generally might be much better at understanding things on an intellectual, rather than an emotional level, and I think it is this understanding that can help us enormously when we are trying to cope with the changes we ourselves are experiencing. The life of a woman changes forever after pregnancy and childbirth, and the physical symptoms and scars of this are ever present, and a constant reminder of the process. I think knowing this, and keeping this at the forefront of our minds as men, will help us adjust to any changes we might find difficult.

As men, I think we **know** our lives will be different when we become fathers, but the problem is that women have a nine month head start. Our lives may not **feel** much different until we have a baby in our arms and everything has changed. Then we need to adjust quickly, and bearing in mind things like the content of this chapter can help with that process.

SEVEN
FATHERHOOD AND SACRIFICE

In the previous chapter, we spent some time considering some of the sacrifices a woman makes during pregnancy and childbirth and some of the ways their lives change once they experience motherhood. The main goal of looking at those issues was to provide a foundation for helping you cope with fatherhood, as this will inevitably lead to changes in your own life. This chapter will focus on how you can come to terms with your changing life, what those changes might include, and how best to adjust to your new life as a father.

In today's world, the sacrifice of our own needs and wants is not a popular idea. Instead, we are encouraged by society to live our lives our way, to put ourselves first, and do what feels good in the moment. The only problem with this attitude is that, at least as far as fatherhood is concerned, that approach has never worked in any generation in world history to date. It is unlikely to start working now, or when you become a father.

When it comes to pregnancy, women have something of a head start. They will **literally** feel the difference almost immediately, whereas, for many men, the first time the responsibility **feels** real is when there's a baby in their arms and they're sitting next to a very sweaty person in the delivery suite.

This gives us men a bit of a problem—how do we very quickly adjust to having to prioritise another person, and how do we do this without being grumpy with everyone around us, particularly the mother of our child? This is why this chapter is helpful land important—it will help you to start to navigate this tricky process and reduce the chances of significant problems.

When fatherhood arrives, your life will be different, this much at least should be very clear by now. However, this daunting prospect can leave you worrying that whilst there are new things you can enjoy now which you will love, there will be a whole list of things you think you cannot do anymore. The truth is that this is rarely the case. One of things that I found helpful when I was a new father was to focus on the fact that, actually, childhood is a series of shorter stages, and that as your child develops and learns, their needs change too.

I remember sitting at my daughter's bedside for two hours waiting for her to drop off to sleep (I know, bad parenting!); I found it very hard work and found myself feeling quite annoyed about having to sacrifice that time. I consoled myself by focusing on the fact that this was only likely to be necessary for a set period of time, not forever.

This was proved true when a few months later my daughter had reached the age where we could explain that it wasn't helpful for me to sit there for that long, and, to my amazement, bedtime started to only take fifteen minutes! Obviously, this whole situation could have been avoided with a different approach from the start, but the point I'm making remains valid. Particularly tricky periods that require significant sacrifices tend to be temporary, not a permanent state of affairs.

I learned that by telling myself that I was temporarily deprioritising some of the things I used to love to do just for me, I felt much more positive and able to accept the 'forced changes' in my life. If I focused on all the things I was missing and told myself I could never do anything I wanted to again, the stress would probably have broken me! Thinking in this new way also frees you up to take pleasure in what you're doing and fatherhood more generally, rather than it feeling like a freedom-stealing inconvenience. I also taught myself to focus on the good parts of the role I didn't enjoy. I've never liked changing poo-filled nappies, but I focused on the fact that I didn't want my daughter sitting in her own mess, and I felt more motivated to see it as a good thing to do.

I can find playing with my daughter quite difficult at times, because the games she plays are, unsurprisingly, not very stimulating for an adult male. However, I cope with the sacrifice I'm making (through doing this instead of what I want to do) by **enjoying her enjoyment**. What I mean by this is that I focus on how much she is enjoying our shared activity, and her laughs and giggles keep me wanting to carry on.

That's the 'carrot' element of my thinking. The 'stick' part of my thinking is that I never want my daughter to think she is not important to me, or that I don't have time for her. That is a slightly more unpleasant way of thinking, but it is a powerful motivator when it needs to be. The things that you may do less as a father—hobbies, interests, time with friends—are not sacrifices in the normal sense. You get to keep them, perhaps just engage with them less frequently, or not at all for a period of time. What you're gaining during the time you're not doing these other things are parenting skills and an active cultivation of a relationship with your child that is unique. I can honestly say I have never regretted choosing to prioritise my daughter over something else I could have done instead.

This chapter is not a magic wand, and it never sought to be. What I think this chapter helps to remind us is that there are a number of sacrifices that come with fatherhood, and that these can be difficult to cope with. The trick to coping with sacrifice is tied up in how we think about our sacrifices.

If we remind ourselves that these sacrifices are temporary, not permanent, and if we focus on finding joy from the things we now 'have' to do with our children, then the time will go quickly, and you can start to re-introduce the things you had to cut down on (presuming you want to start doing them again, of course). If you can prepare yourself for this process before your child arrives, you'll have a significant head start and can really maximise the positive aspects of fatherhood.

EIGHT
FATHERHOOD AND CHANGING RELATIONSHIPS

Fatherhood is all about relationships. You are starting a brand new relationship with your child, and presuming this is your first child, it's the first time you will experience this very unique type of relationship. Fatherhood often also brings changes to many other relationships in your life. You will probably notice your relationship with your own parents begins to alter slightly as you finally start to see things from their point of view and empathise with the headaches you may have caused them! Friendships are likely to alter, especially if your friends are not parents yet, or have no plans to be parents.

The relationship we're going to focus on here, though, is the relationship with the mother of your child. I'm aware that not all fathers will be in a long-term committed relationship with the mother of their child, so this chapter may feel less relevant to you than some of the other chapters. However, I'm sure there will still be useful information for single fathers in here too.

Fatherhood and parenting can lead to changes in your

relationship with the mother of your child, and as such, you will need to be prepared to manage these changes and adjust to your new relationship. The good news is that the basic rules and recipes for success are the same, but you may need to pay extra attention to some areas than you had to before. At the risk of sounding melodramatic, parenting will test your relationship like nothing else, and if you want to continue having a successful relationship that remains intimate (emotionally and sexually), and parent well, hard work is required.

You may not have been much of a communicator before you became a father, so now is a very good time for that to change. You and your partner will need to talk about all kinds of things that you may not have expected to discuss before. There might be difficult decisions to make. For example, your child may need medical attention, or your child may have extra developmental needs. All of these decisions are made much easier with by open and engaged communication.

You don't need me to tell you that parenting can lead to very strong emotions, which can trigger conflicts and arguments if not managed well. It might not take much before accusations of not taking an equal share of the work, or focusing too much on yourself, can arise. For first-time parents, these pressures can be tricky and the accompanying emotions can spill over and make conversations at these points quite difficult to navigate. Below is a set of steps that you could use to assertively express your feelings. It is called 'I Language', and the emphasis is on *I* rather than *you*, which is what keeps the discussion calm.

. . .

1. Describe the situation factually

"Last night the baby cried four times during the night, and I got up each time to see to him."

2. As calmly as possible, express how the situation left you feeling

"I feel annoyed and disappointed that I was the only one to get up and see to him."

3. Specify what you would like to happen instead

'I'd like it if we took turns seeing to him when he wakes up during the night.'

4. Outcome – what is in it for both of you if you follow the suggested way forward

"That way I won't feel annoyed, and I will be more motivated to help fairly during the day."

Another important aspect of effective communication is the ability to *listen with compassion*. When most people think they're listening, what they might actually be doing is simply waiting to make their own point, rather than actually listening and seeking to empathise. Listening with compassion also involves asking questions to gather more information to make sure we show that we actually care about what we're hearing. This helps the person expressing the problem to feel heard, to have their concerns acknowledged, and it also makes it possible to move on and start to think about possible solutions or ways to address any problems raised.

When fatherhood arrives, you need to get used to appreciating your partner and enjoying them and their company in a different way than before your child arrived. There will be an adjustment period as you come to terms with the fact that being spontaneous about how you spend your time is more complicated. It's not impossible (and don't lose sight of that), it just requires more organisation and flexibility.

This is also true of the physical side of your relationship. Sex is something that may need longer to return to your relationship, and this is normal. It is important that you continue to talk about this with you partner and be patient with each other. Pregnancy and childbirth can have a huge impact on a woman's body, and they are likely to take a while to feel 'normal' again, and this is likely to impact on how interested they are in sex. It's important to remain physical though, as a complete absence of affection can be unhelpful in itself for many reasons. Staying affectionate (but not necessarily sexual) will help you to continue to feel emotionally and physically close to your partner.

The good news is that your partner has a chance to see a side of you that they may not have seen before—your more nurturing side. Many women talk about falling in love with their partner all over again, as they come to appreciate aspects of their partner's personality that were previously hidden from their view, but that are very much centre stage with the advent of fatherhood. You too may also see a side of your partner you haven't seen before. The process of giving birth is incredible to witness, and you will see your partner in a new light, working through an incredible situation that requires physical and psychological strength and bravery.

When there is a baby on the scene, your relationship dynamics can shift quite suddenly. Mothers can feel like they are no longer the centre of attention as a pregnant person, and they may now feel like they are simply a feeding machine for the baby, and no longer a person in their own right. As for men, we need to prepare for not being the centre of our partner's world, and sometimes this can feel threatening, and some men can even experience feelings of jealousy towards their child, particularly initially. Coping with this is going to be made easier by talking to each other regularly and ensuring that your partner still feels like a person in their own right.

Parenting can also be a threat to your relationship. Many couples who rarely argued before they became parents can find themselves suddenly transformed into squabbling, sniping wrecks, finding new ways to irritate each other and pick holes in what the other is doing. In some extreme cases, couples can decide that they simply cannot live together and parent, or that this new experience has taught them they are not right for each other.

This is why valuing and protecting you relationship is so important after the arrival of a baby. It can be so easy to let your relationship absent-mindedly slip down your list of priorities, especially when there are suddenly all these new other important things to worry about. Actually, it is through times like these, when you're both likely to be stressed and vulnerable, when you need each other, and a strong and mutually respectful relationship the most.

In summary, becoming a father will probably coincide with some significant changes in your relationship with you partner. Some of these changes are unavoidable, and others can be avoided with some planning and open discussions with your partner. It is important to remember that a change in your relationship at this point is normal, and it would probably be slightly unusual to notice no changes at all in your relationship. The key is patience and working together to work through any problems respectful as a team (covered in more detail in Chapter 11).

NINE
MANAGING RESENTMENT

This chapter will deal mainly with the issue of resentment. As stated throughout this book, parenthood and, in your case, fatherhood, is a wonderful experience. However, it is a life changing process, and not all of the changes that will occur in your life will feel positive, especially in the early days. The fact that you may experience less than positive emotions as a result of these changes, means that you are vulnerable to feelings of resentment, which, if left unmanaged, can lead to stronger feelings of frustration and perhaps even anger. This is why it is important that any feelings of resentment are identified quickly, so that you can start to put things in place and not allow your feelings to escalate and to ensure that you can be the attentive and happy father you would like to be.

So, what do we mean by resentment then? Well, we're referring to consistent feelings of annoyance, irritation, frustration, animosity, or anger. Feelings of resentment can make us irritable, snappy, very grumpy, and it also means that we spend our time thinking about all the things we feel unable to do that we used to enjoy so much. This can mean that we are not focusing on being the type of father we want to be, and that can cause problems in relationships and in other areas of our lives.

I like to think of resentment as the grumpy cousin of 'FOMO' (fear of missing out). Another problem with resentment is that it lingers, and it can impact on how open minded you are when you face a new situation. For example, if you feel resentful towards your partner because you feel they have not thought about you as much as they should, you may lean towards adopting a more self-focused view next time there are negotiations and discussions to be had.

There are a number of reasons we might end up feeling resentment. It might be the case that we were too passive when trying to work through a problem and ended up feeling hard done by because of the outcome. We can feel resentful if we think our thoughts and feelings were not considered fairly, or given the respect they should have been. We can also feel resentful if we think our efforts or good work are overlooked, or not taken into account when a decision or judgement is made.

Probably one of the most prevalent reasons for resentment as a new father is feeling that this new role is impinging on your life so much that you cannot do any of the things you used to do, especially as fatherhood can be stressful and sometimes there is less time to do the things that helped up manage our stress levels before! Whatever the reason for feeling resentment, it can really damage our ability to trust others or be genuinely open when exploring ways of solving difficulties we face. It can also make us very unforgiving and harsh when other people get things wrong or make a mistake.

Resentment can undermine our motivation to try to solve problems productively and can also impact our motivation to seek support and company. It leaves you questioning fairness in all manner of situations, and it can also lead to a descent into unhelpful thinking and a negative outlook more generally.

Overcoming Resentment

So, how can we overcome the feelings of resentment that might be interfering with our ability to be the father we want to be then? I think the first step is likely going to be about actually admitting to ourselves that we are struggling with feelings of resentment. This can be quite a tricky thing to do, as we can feel quite guilty or self-indulgent for feeling resentful.

We then need to consider what we can do to help us feel less resentful, and this might include several steps. Firstly, we need to consider what thinking is underpinning the feelings of resentment, and then we need to spend some time trying to evaluate how accurate these beliefs actually are. For example, if we feel resentful because we feel like we have had to give up a lot of our passions, it can be helpful to think about all of the things that our partners have also given up, or how their life has also changed. This sense of not being alone can really help to challenge unhelpful thinking, and, subsequently, the feelings of resentment.

Sometimes, one of the main problems with resentment is that you may feel it is unfair or inappropriate for you to feel this way. In these situations, it can often feel difficult to express these feelings to anyone or share them out loud, for fear of judgement, or to avoid reinforcing our own sense of shame about resentment.

One way of managing this is to write down the thoughts and feelings linked to your resentment. This can be done in a number of ways, but it might be as simple as writing a list. Another option might be to write a letter to the person that you're feeling resentful towards. These documents are not being written to show to anyone, more as a way of expressing yourself and helping to process and rationalise some of the emotions. You may find that once the resentment is written out in front of you, it loses its power and hold over you. After the letter or list is written, it should be destroyed.

Another option is to speak to the person who you think is the reason you're feeling resentful. This involves staying calm and thinking carefully about what are the factual things you can highlight and what might be more about your own preferences. If you feel confident about expressing yourself calmly and fairly, and that you know how things could be different after talking this through with your partner, it could really help to strengthen your relationship. It may be that the person who you are busy feeling resentful towards is not even aware that you are feeling this way. They might be keen to correct things, or at least make sure they don't contribute to you feeling this way again. Of course, they cannot do this if they're not aware of your grievance.

A big part of the process of overcoming resentment links to forgiveness. Ultimately, if you feel that someone has mistreated you, whether that be your partner, or your new child (by impacting on your life in ways you didn't expect, or to a greater extent than you predicted), you need to genuinely forgive them. One way of making it easier for you to forgive someone else is to think about your own role in the situation. If you can find even a small way in which you contributed to the situation, it becomes much easier to assign less of the responsibility and frustration to others. You may need to repeat this process over a number of days to maximise its effectiveness. This part of this process is critical in allowing yourself to genuinely move on from the resentment.

I can vividly remember telling myself that I never wanted my daughter to feel like I didn't have time for her when she needed me. That made it much easier for me to squash feelings of resentment, as there was a greater goal in my mind.

Whichever of the above methods you choose to try to address your resentment, once you have completed these steps, you can invest some time in managing how your life can feel different and lighter without the presence of this resentment.

So, in summary, resentment can be a destructive emotional experience that can negatively impact on your ability to be the father that you want to be. There are a couple of ways of dealing with it, and you may need to repeat these processes to make them work. The important thing is that lots of new fathers experience resentment, and that doesn't make you evil or incredibly selfish. It's a normal part of the adjustment to fatherhood. Be calm but firm with yourself, and you can achieve a gentle determination to push through these feelings and really be the father that you want to be for your child.

PART THREE
GO!

TEN
DAY OF ARRIVAL

This chapter will cover the day your child actually arrives. It won't include details about different types of birth, but instead will focus on what your role is during the big day, and how you can be most helpful to your partner. The day your child is born will be like no other. From the moment your child is born, you will have a new set of responsibilities that will feel quite heavy, but you will also experience a type of love that is totally unique and special.

As the father, your role in this momentous event can take many shapes and forms, and they can be very different, based on your own preferences and those of your partner. Some men like to get very involved and be with their partner every step of the way, even getting into the birthing pool with their partner. Not all men will want this (and sometimes their partner won't either). There are no rights or wrongs in terms of what your involvement looks like on the day, but it is useful to spend a bit of time thinking about and talking to your partner about what is right for the both of you.

I'm quite a squeamish person, and tend to feel quite uncomfortable in hospitals, but I was determined to be with my wife during every step of the process. I felt she didn't have a choice about going through the process, so I should be there with her (and she agreed with this view). This meant that I sat next to her as they performed the caesarean section, and I did my best to hold her hand and talk to her as the procedure was happening, despite mostly feeling anxiety and worrying about fainting. My wife, of course, was a trooper and managed the whole process in a much more stoic way than I did.

There are things to think about before the time comes that would be useful investments of your time and attention.

Birth Plan

Labour and childbirth can be quite unpredictable. With this in mind, it would be useful for you to be very familiar with your partner's birth plan. The doctors and nurses at the time may have questions about your partner's preferences, and it would be very helpful for you to be able to discuss important issues about your partner's preferences, so you can be informed on the day, and unexpected changes in the process can be responded to as calmly as possible, without too many surprises.

Jokes

. . .

Lots of men deal with difficult feelings or stressful situations through humour. Now, you know your partner better than I do, and it is not my place to tell you not to try and be funny during labour. What I would say though, is that your partner is likely to feel a high degree of stress and anxiety, so jokes should be cracked only after careful consideration. She needs a supportive and confident helping hand, not a stand-up comedian. Remember that what might seem hilarious to you at the time (and possibly to her at a different time) might be terrifying and anxiety provoking during and around childbirth.

Pack a Bag

There will be a lot of talk of your partner having a bag ready to go to the hospital, but you should have one too. It should include snacks for both of you, something to entertain you—a good book or two probably—spare clothes, and a few toiletries. Labour can be stressful, and it could be worse if you're uncomfortable, hungry, or bored.

Prepare for the Unexpected

Labour and childbirth is hard to roadmap definitively. It is important that you know your partner's preferences and have discussed these beforehand. You may also need to discuss how you can support your partner in different scenarios, as well as what to do if your partner does not respond the way you expect. Given this is a unique experience that is quite rare, don't be surprised if your partner does not act in the way she said she would—a lot can change at very short notice. You may need to have a few different techniques up your sleeve.

Often, fathers can be caught off-guard, or even a little scared, when their partner makes different noises during childbirth than they have ever made before. If you prepare yourself for this eventuality, then you can concentrate on supporting your partner, rather than scratching your head with a confused expression on your face, or hiding behind a curtain. This is probably the time when she needs you the most, so make sure you're present, even if you're feeling unsure or anxious. Try not to get caught up in how your partner is treating you; she is under stress, and your job is to be there for her. She is unlikely to be focused on perspective taking whilst she is giving birth.

Watching Birth

For several reasons, some men may feel uncomfortable watching the actual birth. They may be squeamish (like myself), they may not want to worry about watching something up close that is hurting their partner, or they may worry that they will want sex less after they watch a birth. This is definitely a discussion topic with your partner. You need to decide between the two of you what will maximise enjoyment and reduce anxiety or stress during birth.

. . .

Coaching/Cheerleading

The reality of the situation is that there is often little you can do during childbirth. Don't feel too downbeat if your role feels quite minor, and you find yourself simply sitting next to her mopping her brow and telling her she's doing great. Often, that's the most powerful thing you can do. Your partner will need your support and presence, possibly more than they ever have before, so don't diminish the importance of these small, simple, and supportive acts.

Debrief

You may need to talk to someone about what you have just witnessed after your child is born. Arrange with someone to debrief (preferably a father who has already experienced what you just have) and think about talking things through with them. You might want to prepare them for the fact that you might call at 4 a.m. having been asked to leave the hospital for the night, and you're having racing thoughts about the birth. You've been supporting your partner through a difficult process, now it's time for you to access some support for yourself—your wellbeing matters too.

In summary, labour and childbirth can be a very unique but very challenging time. Remember that you will have a whole set of feelings about these processes, and your partner is likely to feel them in greater intensity. The best you can do is just be there to offer support, and this should be driven by your partner's needs. If you can, try to enjoy it. It is a unique process that some men never get to experience, so make the most of it and be the best teammate you can be for your partner.

ELEVEN
TEAMWORK MAKES THE DREAM WORK

So, it's happened, you're a father! Congratulations! But what's next? Well there's a lot of hard work and a lot of joy to come. There's also going to be a period of time where you and your partner settle into a new lifestyle, where you both find your feet as parents. As covered in Chapter 8, your relationship is likely to be different now. These changes are often great, but, initially, they can feel threatening or unexpected. So, it's best to start thinking about these changes and planning for them now.

The main difference you may notice is an increase in the amount of assistance and support you will need to give each other. Parenthood is a shared experience, but not everyone is prepared for this change. So, as the title of this chapter suggests, the focus here is on how you can support each other in a way that benefits both of you and, of course, your child.

It should be no surprise by now that in this chapter I'm going to talk about the benefits of teamwork, and what this actually looks like in practical terms. When my wife was pregnant, a friend who had become a father not long before talked to me about how he had adjusted better to fatherhood once he began to view himself and his partner as teammates working towards a shared goal. This might seem obvious, and in many ways it is. Ask yourself though, when it comes to shared objectives that you and your partner have, how often do you actually ***behave*** in a way that suggests you truly consider them as a joined responsibility?

For example, many men would agree that there is no reason that they should not take their child out alone. However, this is considered more widely in society as quite unusual. I recall taking my daughter alone to a musical parent and baby session, and a couple of the mothers there were absolutely astounded that I took her out on my own. To me it seemed a very normal thing to do, but they explained that their partners would be very unlikely to do such a thing. The point I'm making is that often there is a disconnect between what we ***think*** and what we actually ***do***. This is cognitive dissonance.

So, whilst we can all sit around as fathers and agree that we are just as responsible for parenting as our partners, how often do we actually behave in a way that supports or evidences this thinking? I'm just as guilty of this as the next person. I will often agree with my wife that we should both be doing all of the work parenting requires, but I still find myself waiting for her to do things that there is no reason I couldn't do. It's not laziness, or apathy, it's just me not being mindful of and challenging my dissonance and possibly my underlying stereotypes. I want to walk the walk, not just talk the talk—but to do that requires constant effort and attention.

Communication

. . .

This has been covered a lot in this book already, but it's worth mentioning here. If you were to watch any successful sports team playing, you would see a theme. The ones that succeed the most, or recover from a mistake quickly showing resilience, are the teams that have players talking to each other. In those teams, mouths move just as much as arms and legs, and that is because they understand the importance of good communication to successful teamwork and, consequently, achieving shared objectives.

So, we can all agree that communication is crucial. Now we need to think about how we communicate. Being new parents tends to go hand in hand with exhaustion, which can mean that sometimes communication is not as calm and reasonable as it could be. If there is tension in the team, it is probably best to agree to discuss flash points a little later, when you're both calmer. Before you get to the discussion, try to think about your partner's point of view and find a piece of the 'blame pie' you can take without feeling too resentful. Often, we can take responsibility for something, however small, and doing this helps the other person to feel comfortable taking some responsibility, and this can really take the heat out of difficult conversations.

Another useful approach is to try not to blame or criticise your partner. You may need to make some points, but how you do this is important. For example, rather than 'You know that when you do that it annoys me,' try, 'I find it much easier to cope with those situations when you give me a bit more notice.' This helps to highlight what you would like to happen without increasing the chances of your partner becoming defensive.

. . .

Doing Your Fair Share

We're all different. This means that we all have different approaches to things like housework and jobs that always need doing around the house. You may already be quite proactive in terms of these activities, or you may not. If you're not, this transition into fatherhood may feel a little more difficult. The bottom line is that you are going to need to contribute. If you already do, this might just be a case of picking up a few extra child-related jobs that were not needed before.

If, however, you tended to not do much around the house, you will need to start discussing this with your partner before the baby arrives. Initially, while you make the transition, it might be reasonable for you to have a few jobs that belong solely to you, and over time that can shift so that the split in responsibility between you and your partner is as equal as it reasonably can be. This probably makes sense to most men, but if it doesn't, remember that whatever your child *sees* is how they will learn how you manage in a relationship. If you have a daughter and you want her to be treated with respect as an adult by her partner, start making sure you're doing the same to her mother as soon as she can see and hear, because that's when she starts learning.

You might be a bit like me. I've always been willing to do my fair share, but I'm not the most alert when it comes to proactively noticing opportunities to be helpful and make a contribution. I've got much better over the years, because I have a patient wife who is happy to gently point out these opportunities to be helpful to me, meaning that I've started to spot them myself now.

I appreciate that getting to this point is a journey. One way of managing this is to agree that a set of jobs are your responsibility to manage on a regular basis (e.g. washing clothes). Make a list of your jobs and get used to crossing things off as you do them. This helps you to feel you are contributing, and it also keeps you on track and reduces the chances of you forgetting what you have agreed to do. There are lots of 'to do list' apps which can help with this.

If you both agree which jobs you are each responsible for, you could display an organiser/planner somewhere in your home you will both see. This makes you both a bit more accountable and reduces the chances for conflict, as you can both see who is responsible for what, and when those things should happen. Over time, you'll be surprised how helping out becomes second nature, and your partner will certainly appreciate the support.

Sleep Agreements

Picture the scene. It's three o'clock in the morning and both you and your partner are exhausted having been deprived of sleep for several weeks now. You have both been woken by the baby crying. Initially, in our house, this led to something of a game of 'bed chicken,' where we would both wait to see who cracked first and got out of bed, leaving the other person with a brief sense of delight and then a bigger sense of guilt. When we finally bit the bullet and talked about it, we laughed about the fact we had been doing this and discussed a plan.

We agreed that we would take turns getting out of bed to see to our daughter. It wasn't a great plan, as tiredness helped us to be confused about whose turn it actually was. Then we decided we would alternate entire nights. That worked better for us, and it's one option you can try. We also agreed that I would get up early on Saturday allowing my wife to have a lie in, and that she would do the same for me on Sunday. That way we both had one lie in a week to look forward to.

The harsh and unavoidable reality is that you will both be tired. That is not going to change, but I can assure you it is much easier to cope with feeling tired if you know your partner is also tired and is not taking advantage of your good nature to get a few more hours sleep. As with most topics in this book, communication is key. Agree to a plan and then try it out. If you don't think it's working, don't be afraid to chuck the plan out and try a new one. Trial and error will get you to a point where you are both satisfied with what is happening.

Parental Decision Making

It is likely that there will be times in the coming weeks, months, and years where you and your partner will have different views about parenting that could cause conflicts. Disagreement is normal, but it can quickly become unhealthy if one of you becomes 'the expert' and the other ends up feeling ignored or dismissed and feels their confidence waning.

A joined-up approach is almost certainly the right way forward. Spend some time outlining your views and try to find common ground. Once you've done that, you can hone in on the points of disagreement, and it's often easier to find a middle ground that leaves both of you feeling valued and included. Part of this might involve acceptance that you and your partner have different ways of looking after your child, but, as long as they're safe and there's nothing fundamentally damaging about different approaches, that's okay.

Time

One of the most obvious and quickly noticeable consequences of parenting is the reduction of available time—that's time for you by yourself, as well as time for you and your partner to be alone together. This might seem obvious, but it's worth thinking about a little in advance so you're not firefighting when the time comes. Remember, the happier you are, the more likely you are to be happy in your role as a parent as well.

The truth is that it is unlikely you will have as much free time as you did before, at least initially. So, the best approach is likely to involve trying to incorporate this time into your new-look lifestyle as a parent. So, rather than a night out for dinner and the cinema, it might be a takeaway and a DVD instead. Or, it might be having friends round to spend time with you more, instead of going out to a pub. You may need to get creative to find ways of spending time together and relaxing, but it really is worth the effort.

. . .

Forgiveness

Parenting is very hard work, and it can be very stressful. Go easy on each other and be kind to yourselves. You'll make mistakes and get things wrong, as will your partner. People very rarely do things wrong on purpose, so if your partner makes a mistake, treat it as such, a genuine mistake that was probably due to exhaustion rather than a deliberate effort to cause harm or problems. Imagine how you would want to be spoken to or dealt with after a mistake, and then take that approach with your partner. Ask yourself, is it worth the argument, or is it better just to let it go and earn the same kindness when you've made the mistake?

In summary, life changes once you become a father. It can feel very challenging, which is why some teamwork is so important. The mother of your child is likely to feel similar to you in many ways, which is why working together is so crucial. There are a number of issues to bear in mind as outlined above, but ultimately the take-home message here is that the more you commit to treating your partner as a teammate, the easier this process will feel.

TWELVE
PRACTICAL & EMOTIONAL SUPPORT

We've talked about the importance of teamwork, and how this can help to ensure that both you and the mother of your child work together to stay healthy and as happy as you can. Parenting will test the most patient of people, and that is why having each other to rely on is so useful. A significant part of this is about the support you can offer each other, so this chapter will focus on the issues around support and how best to make sure you can offer your partner the support they need.

Support seems like a very straightforward concept to understand, but there are many people who don't always give support the thought that is necessary. For some, support means offering to do the odd load of washing, whereas, for others it means endless cups of tea and hours of listening while your significant other whiles away the hours crying. Support is sometimes these things, but it is rarely the same thing every time you need to give support to someone else you care about.

So, what is support then? Well we know it can come in

practical and emotional forms, but the complicating factor is that often the same person will want and need different types of support at different times. I do think there are a couple of important components that are always likely to be needed in terms of support. These are **active listening** and **time**.

The need for support is not something that can always be time-tabled in. You won't always know in advance when you'll be required to give support. This means that you may need to make the tough choice to sacrifice something at short notice (which can be really difficult) in order to free up time to support your partner.

I have found this difficult in the past, but I have come to learn that the consequences of not making this choice are often more difficult to cope with than the consequences of making the sacrifice. It's not for me to tell you what to do, obviously, but I would give serious consideration about what consequences you prefer to experience—personal short-term disappointment or potentially significant problems in your relationship that can often take much longer to resolve.

Active listening is also really important. Half-hearted support can often feel more insulting than a complete lack of support, so think about how you are presenting to your partner. Active listening involves making eye contact with your partner and thinking about what they're saying. Asking questions to gather more information can be useful, and empathising is incredibly powerful.

Men are often accused of trying to 'fix' problems, rather than listen to the experience of our partners. I don't think this is because men in general don't care about the feelings of their partners, but because they are driven by a wish to improve things and help their partner feel better. This means they can end up rushing to the solution stage, when actually listening to the problem and the feelings contributes more to helping your partner process those thoughts and feelings, and they will feel validated, listened to, and cared about. Once this initial listening stage has been completed, your partner is likely to be more ready to explore possible solutions with you. The other thing about active listening is that this does not mean simply staying quiet whilst you think about what you're going to say next. Active listening is about genuinely listening.

If the practical support concludes with you needing to do something different, and you promise to do those things, stick to the promises you make. Empty promises are pointless, harmful, and completely undermine your credibility when you next need to try and problem solve with a partner. You just won't be taken seriously. If you're doing something unhelpful, or there are things you could do to better support your partner, do them. You'll feel better, and your partner will appreciate your efforts. You'll also get more slack when things are going wrong elsewhere.

Giving support is not always easy, but remember, it's likely there will be times when you too will need support from a partner. If you have been able to give your partner support, hopefully they will be able to return the favour when it is you who needs some time and help. It can also feel difficult to accept support from a partner, especially if this feels like a new thing to do. As with most things in life, practice makes perfect, so the more you get used to doing this, the more you'll enjoy the benefits of it. You and your partner are a team, so mutual support is a really important part of reinforcing that positive relationship.

This chapter has been about emotional (active listening)

and practical (problem solving) support. We explored the fact that supporting a partner is a choice and requires you to commit to actually listening to and caring about your partner's perspective and the way they're feeling about the challenges they're struggling with at that time. The best approach is often to give emotional support before moving onto more practical problem solving. Taking this approach is likely to yield the best results, and it will really help your partner to see that you want to help them and are serious about this role.

THIRTEEN

EMOTIONAL MANAGEMENT

This chapter is about emotional management. We have already covered the fact that becoming a father can be a stressful process and that there are going to be times your patience will be tested. You may find yourself becoming angry or frustrated, and this can be made much more difficult to manage when you add in high levels of tiredness, anxiety, and sleep deprivation. Even the most placid of men can be pushed to the limit in terms of frustration tolerance when they're holding a screaming baby at half past three in the morning having had one hour of sleep, not been able to engage in the activity that helps them de-stress, and knowing that there is a lot to do at work later.

So, why should we care about this then? Well, emotional management is important for the wellbeing of everyone who shares the home of the child. There are few things worse than the regret you can end up feeling after losing your temper, and when you have lost your temper with your child, the guilt afterwards can be really difficult to process, and you can end up beating yourself up for a long time.

I remember an occasion when my daughter was very young and I reached my limit. I ended up putting her on the floor and walking away. My wife was there so she picked her up and took over from me, but that small act left me feeling very guilty and unhappy about how I had (or had not) managed things. The consequences in this instance were very minor—no physical harm came to anyone, and the only emotional harm was my own guilt. Working in the field I have, I know of very sad cases where the consequences of parents not managing their emotions has led to significant and life changing consequences.

How can we manage our emotions and make sure we're not causing problems for ourselves or our families? The first step is to know when we're starting to lose control of our emotions, and this is often preceded by physical reactions in our bodies, known as *arousal cues*. These cues tell us that we're starting to experience changes in our emotional response. Look at the list below:

- Feeling hot
- Rapid heart beat
- Rapid breathing
- Tense muscles (e.g. tight shoulders, clenching fists)
- Sweating
- Having a dry mouth/throat
- Trembling or shaking
- Knot in stomach
- Speaking quickly

It is likely that you will find some of the above cues familiar as you experience one of more of them yourself when you know you're starting to feel angry or irritated. Knowing your own physical cues is the first step to effective emotional management. When you notice your personal cues are present, then you can start to use emotional management strategies to intervene and reduce your levels of emotional response. Many books have been written about emotional management and the topic is vast. Below I have included some quick techniques you can use to reduce those feelings before they lead to problems.

- Meditation/Mindfulness/Relaxation Techniques

These types of techniques are helpful for many people, and they are well worth trying. The added advantage is that they are free and often immediately accessible. The main goal is to focus on your breathing and nothing else. This will help you to clear your mind, which can, in itself, help to take the sting out of difficult emotions. You will obviously need to make sure that someone else is caring for your child while you're doing this. But, if you try to find a few minutes to do this every day, you may find yourself surprised at how much it helps you to remain calm.

- Ask for help

If you feel you have reached your limit, the safest and best thing you can do for your child might be just to reach out and ask someone to step in. Even half an hour away from your child will allow you to unwind enough to feel ready to return. If your partner is not available for whatever reason, are their friends and/or family who you could contact and have some respite?

After I returned to work after paternity leave, my wife would regularly arrive at my father's house and hand our daughter over for an hour while she had a cup of tea. It was a simple act, but it made a huge difference to her wellbeing. Perhaps there is someone you could have 'on call' in those early months/years. People won't necessarily know you could do with the help, so they may not offer, but they would actually be more than happy to help.

Of course you are likely to also have the mother of your child available to talk to. This is your primary teammate, so don't forget to talk to them about how you're feeling. They can empathise and will probably share some of your frustrations. It helps enormously not to feel alone at these times.

- Regular exercise

Exercise is great for stress management and emotional regulation. Even going for walks can be great to help de-stress, and it's a great family activity that helps you all get some fresh air, de-stress, and spend time together working as a team.

- Manage your thinking

This book has often talked about the expectations and realities of parenthood. Once I had got my head around the fact that things were going to be difficult for a period of time, but that this would change in the future, fatherhood became much easier for me to cope with. It can still be difficult even now, but when I tell myself that this tricky phase won't last forever, it's much easier for me to feel less angry or stressed by it.

This chapter has highlighted the important role of emotional management in fatherhood. The techniques covered here are quite basic, but they can be very powerful. Once you come to learn your physical cues, you can start to intervene by trying some of the suggestions above, or by doing things that you know work for you, to help you stay on top of those difficult feelings and stress levels. Managing your emotions will help you to be the father you want to be, and it will also help to ensure that you are modelling effective emotional management to your child.

FOURTEEN

TIMETABLING AND PLANNING

As the title suggests, this chapter is focused on quite practical aspects of life as a father, particularly in those early days after the arrival of your child. As we have already covered in this book, how you spend your time is going to change once you are a father, and some of those activities will be really enjoyable, and others will be less fun. We have covered the need to be realistic about your expectations of how much free time you will have and how much access to the activities that you used to enjoy you will have.

Timetabling and planning are going to be very important at this point. You and your partner will both have individual activities that you would like to engage in, as well as wanting to spend time together, and normal daily commitments, such as work. These activities can be even more important as a way of de-stressing, which, as we covered in the previous chapter, is very helpful given the emotional demands of parenthood that can be challenging to manage.

You and the mother of your child may already be planners, which is going to make this approach fairly easy to adapt to parenthood. If you are not currently planners, then trying this approach is going to be very helpful, and, hopefully, something of a revelation! It's not a complicated process, but basically involves you sitting down once a week with your partner and trying to forecast what your time commitments are over the next week or two.

Doing this exercise together has a number of advantages. Firstly, both of you will feel involved and consulted, and it will reinforce the sense of teamwork that is so important (as covered in Chapter 11). It also means that you have a deeper understanding of what is important to your partner and their priorities, which reduces the chances of unnecessary resentment and misunderstandings. Simply run through each day and make a note of the big tasks that need doing. The next priority is then to find and agree some time to spend together (if you are in a relationship with the mother of your child). If there is any time to spare after this, you might choose to engage in individual activities or interests.

The above approach will help achieve a sense of fairness and ensure that you do have time together, which is crucial to keeping the lines of communication open. As this time is being 'reserved,' it means that you know there will be opportunities to talk about how you're feeling and anything you're struggling with, and you can check in with your partner to see how she is managing and feeling about how things are working.

Another advantage to this approach is that if you're having a tricky moment, you know that there's some time coming up when you're going to be able to do something you're looking forward to, and this can be a godsend when emotions are high and stress levels are really pushed. I would find myself thinking "This is really difficult, and I'm so bored with sitting here while she tries to sleep, but at least I know I'm going to go out running tomorrow night." I cannot tell you how much being able to think like that helped in the moment.

Now, you might be reading this thinking that it sounds awful, and it's just a way of removing any spontaneity out of your life. To an extent, planning this way does limit (but not totally remove) chances for spontaneity. You do not have to adopt this approach forever. I'm suggesting that it is a useful thing to do whilst you navigate through the first year or so of your child's life. You may learn that as time passes you can be a bit more relaxed about this approach, but I do think it's invaluable at the start, just as a way of helping you feel grounded and ensuring that you still have the ability to engage in activities in your life that you really enjoyed and could do freely before parenthood.

So, timetabling and planning is a really useful tool when it comes to managing the stresses and strains of parenthood. This is a good thing to talk to a partner about. It demonstrates that you're thinking about these issues. Also, the fact that you want to protect some time to spend with your partner will help her to feel valued. Women can often feel that once they become mothers they lose their identity as an individual, as the focus can shift totally to the child. They can end up feeling like no more than So and so's mummy.

Through planning, you can let her know that she is still all the things to you she was before she was a mother. She will also be pleased that you consider it important that she has a bit of time to herself. I think this is something I could have done better when my daughter arrived, so please learn from my mistakes and make sure your partner has some time to unwind alone! Planning and timetabling is a little bit more work for many important benefits, and it is well worth the time investment.

PART FOUR
FATHERHOOD

FIFTEEN

BONDING

This chapter moves on to consider fatherhood more broadly, and how you can maximise the positive impact that you can have on your child (or children). Fatherhood can be a multifaceted exercise, and this can mean that engagement can happen on a number of levels. It is possible to be a good practical father, by earning money and making sure your child is fed and clothed and has all the practical things they need to function. Being a father who provides emotional support and warmth is a different level, and this requires more engagement beyond physical needs.

Issues around attachment and bonding are important for a number of reasons. In the early days, your child is clearly completely reliant on you and their mother (and any other caregivers) to literally survive, so they will naturally start to bond with you the more you engage in these activities. Bonding is important because the closer your child feels to you as they grow up and develop, physically and emotionally, then the more effective you will be able to be as a father. This means you will have more respect and credibility in their eyes, and it will also mean the relationship is more rewarding and enjoyable for both of you. So, how can we achieve this bonding? Below are some things to consider:

Start Early

A baby can hear from within the womb from around 18 weeks. They are becoming used to the voices of you and their mother, so try talking to the baby and engaging with it. Now I know this can feel a bit silly, but if it helps, and if you're not sure what to say, try reading a story or reciting nursery rhymes. It's really about helping the baby get used to your voice. Your partner is also likely to notice that your child responds to your voice by kicking and moving about, and this can be a really nice thing to experience for all of you.

Skin to skin contact

If possible, as soon as you can after they're born, get some skin on skin contact with your child. It might be worth including this in the birth plan and letting the midwives who are present know, so that you're not forgotten in all of the activity around birth. Skin-to-skin contact lets your baby hear your heartbeat and learn your smell, just like they do with their mother if they're breastfeeding. Take every opportunity you can to let them snuggle up on your chest. It's a really nice way to feel close, and it can help you both relax too.

. . .

A Dad Only Activity

One nice way of bonding is to find an activity that only *you* do with your child. This might include baby massage sessions, which also encourages physical contact, or attending a musical session. Often, I would take my daughter to a musical session on my own, and I really enjoyed that half hour as something special that the two of us regularly did together. The added bonus was that my wife got a bit of time to herself to relax and do other bits that needed doing.

Comforting

It's important for you as the father to be involved in soothing your child. So when they're upset, try to make sure it's just as likely that you will pick them up and help them feel better. You might do this by hugging them or comforting them with your voice and reassuring them. I got into the habit of singing 'Moonshadow' to my daughter when she got upset. Now she is used to this song, and it helps her feel calmer and less distressed quite quickly, and she is just as likely to seek me out when she is upset as she is her mother.

Bedtime Routine

There are many baby books that talk about the importance of a consistent routine and bed time, and this is conventional wisdom that I have no plans to argue with. I'm more interested in your role in this important process. It might be that you could take part of it (maybe a bath or reading a story), and this can be something that is your job, and that can contribute to the bonding process. Routines are very helpful with children and family life in general, and can really help everyone feel settled as they know what to expect. Consistency is key.

Caring for your child when they are unwell

It is useful for fathers to take time off work to care for sick children, just as much as it is for mothers. This helps them learn that your role is also about nurturing and caring, and they can come to you for help if they feel unwell or just want some TLC.

Rough and tumble

One type of play that dads seem to be particularly skilled at is rough and tumble. That's the bouncing on the knee, aeroplane around the room, and some tickling. From around six months old, your child will love all of this. As it's a fun activity for both of you, there will be plenty of feel good dopamine around for both of you too. It will not only help you to bond, it will also help to improve your child's co-ordination and core body strength, so it's wins all round!

. . .

In summary, your bond with your child is fundamentally important to your successful and effective relationship moving forward. Above are some basic things you can start to do almost as soon as your partner becomes pregnant to start working on this bond. It can be easy to just assume that the mother-child bond is the only important one, but this is a myth. Evolution has ensured that the bonds fathers have with their children are different from the bonds they have with their mothers, and this helps to prepare children for the range of people they will encounter throughout their lives.

SIXTEEN

MODELLING

In this final chapter, we'll spend some time considering another important aspect of fatherhood—modelling. When we talk about modelling, we are referring to the way that you behave in front of your children, because as soon your child is born, you are in effect modelling (or demonstrating) to them how to do things. They learn how to use cutlery, walk, talk, solve problems, and interact with other people, all through this modelling process.

So much of what children learn is through observation and listening to you. Sometimes this is deliberate—you might choose to teach your child how to ride a bike by practicing balancing skills, etc. However, children learn *all* the time, when we mean them to and when we don't. This means that they're twenty-four-hours-a-day learners, always watching and listening to us as parents, soaking up the experiences they have with us.

This is why phrases like 'practice what you preach' are so powerful. If you want your children to behave in certain ways or do certain things, you need to show them how and why they should do that. Ask yourself the question, how much respect do you have for people who say they will do things, and then do something completely different? They have no credibility. If you want your child to respect and follow your wishes, you need to show them that you behave the right way, even when you think they're not looking (and they probably are, by the way!).

Studies have demonstrated that positive involvement from fathers can have profound effects on children. This can be in terms of physical wellbeing, perceptual ability, and social skills when interacting with other people. Additionally, the studies appear to suggest that children with a positive father role model take initiative more naturally, and also have increased self-control abilities.

Self-Esteem and Body Image

Fathers play a key role in the psychological development of their children. Children with disengaged or absent fathers tend to have lower levels of self-esteem, whereas children who have fathers present are more likely to develop a strong sense of self and feel more confident in themselves and their abilities.

Body image can also be impacted on by positive fathers, especially when it comes to daughters. When fathers show their partners and daughters unconditional love, and do not comment on the physical aspects of women they encounter, they are helping to foster a lifelong positive body image, as well as showing daughters how they should expect to be treated as adults, and teaching sons how to respect women.

. . .

Persistence

Fathers can greatly increase the chances that their children learn how to be resilient, and be motivated to persist, even when things get tricky. A father who provides warmth and love, alongside accountability to rules and responsibility, is helping his children learn about persistence. According to researcher Laura Padilla-Walker, 'fathers who are most effective are those who listen to their children, have a close relationship, set appropriate rules, but also grant appropriate freedoms.'

Behavioural Traits

Psychology used to put a heavily biased emphasis on the bond between a mother and her children, but recent studies have shown that a father also has a great influence on his children—as well as their mother—when it comes to the development of behavioural traits. Fathers who show love to their children and accept them as they are help foster a positive sense of self. Negligent fathers, on the other hand, run the risk of increasing the chances of their child experiencing depression, substance abuse, and psychological problems.

Social Skills

. . .

Fathers who communicate well and respectfully with others help their children to do the same, and the children learn about the rules of interaction with other people. This will also help your children learn how to talk about their thoughts and feelings, and this increased emotional intelligence is extremely powerful in contributing to adult successes in a number of fields.

Positive Relationships

Fathers teach their children how to interact with partners in relationships. From an early age, children pick up on the way their fathers treat women, typically their mothers. Fathers who are abusive (verbally or non-verbally), neglectful or hurtful towards their spouses are unknowingly teaching their children how partners deserve to be treated. Many women who find themselves in abusive relationships later in life report some form of abuse, or witnessing such abuse, as a child, even if it is a minor occurrence. Fathers who show love to their partners and children teach them that partners should be treated with respect, loved and cared for by others in their lives.

The point of this chapter was not to terrify you into thinking that any single misstep will cause huge psychological damage to your children and ruin their futures. The point I'm making is broader than that. Effectively, you teach your children everything, so you need to think about the things you want your children to learn, and then act accordingly. Things will go wrong sometimes, and that's fine—it is after all a part of the human condition. It also gives you an opportunity to show your children how to recover from setbacks, which is an important skill in itself. This is just a nudge to ask yourself, 'If my child could see me doing this now, what would I be teaching them?'

CONCLUDING THOUGHTS

At the start of this book, I made you a promise.

I promised that if you followed the advice and suggestions in this book, you would be in a much better position to enjoy fatherhood, and cope with the new challenges and changing parts of your life. I promised that you'd be able to do most of it for free, and that it could lead to many benefits and a closer bond between you and the new child in your life. One of the key parts of the promise was that you needed to follow the guidelines and suggestions made in this book.

I'm not going to lie to you and suggest that fatherhood is easy or that this book is a magic wand. However, following the guidelines offered here will be a great start on your journey to enjoying fatherhood and getting the most out of it for you and your child.

I stand by my promise. I am confident that the material in this book can make a big difference in your life and the lives of your family, especially the child or children you are now going to share your life with.

Good luck! Fatherhood is without a doubt the hardest yet single most rewarding experience of my life so far. I know you're going to love it.

REVIEW PLEA

Thank you for buying my book.

I really appreciate all of your feedback, and I love hearing what you have to say.

I need your input to make the next version better, and to help my career as a writer.

Please leave me an honest review on Amazon, or wherever you bought this book.

Also, please feel free to email me your thoughts:
petecblack@gmail.com

Thank you so much!

Peter Black

UNTITLED

Produced by CPW Media Ltd and Nevno Publishing

 The author greatly appreciates you taking the time to read his work. Please consider leaving a review wherever you bought the book, or telling your friends about it, to help spread the word.

Thank you for supporting my work.

ISBN-10:
ISBN-13:

I am on Facebook – https://www.facebook.com/peterblackwriter

I am on Twitter - @petecblack

Please check out my website – www.petercblack.co.uk

CAN THESE OTHER BOOKS HELP?

"Cool That Volcano: How to Help Children Stay Calm, Manage Anger and Master Emotions"

By

Peter Black

Are your children difficult to control? Are you starting to worry that their constant temper tantrums and explosive anger are getting out of hand? You're not alone.

It is a fact that many children experience difficulties in managing their emotions, and can express anger in a damaging way that causes problems for them, and others around them.

This book is packed full of techniques and methods that take you through a step by step approach to teaching your children how to manage their emotions, in a concise and easy to read manner. This is not a 300 page technical manual, but it is a set of practical methods which help you to help your child stay in control of, and master their emotions. This will almost certainly improve their lives, and the lives of those who care about them.

In this guide you'll learn how to:

Teach your child to recognise problematic emotions
Teach your child how to calm down and manage anger
Teach your child how to talk about their feelings
Teach your child how to achieve mastery of their emotions
Think about your own approach to emotional management

What are you waiting for? Read this book, apply the methods inside, and begin to improve your child's life today.

Get the book here – https://books2read.com/u/4Ax5PK

"How to Move House Stress Free: The Step by Step Guide to Moving Home Successfully"

By

Peter Black

Are you considering moving home? Are you starting to worry that the stress of a move is going to push you over the edge, or that you'll make bad decisions?

It is a fact that many people worry about the prospect of a move and whether it is right for them or their families. Many people also worry about the stress that might be cause by moving home.

This book is packed full of techniques and methods that take you through a step by step approach to moving home, in a concise and easy to read manner. This is not a 300-page technical manual, but it is a set of practical methods which help you to navigate the process of moving, from deciding whether to move, to picking up the keys to your new home. This book will almost certainly make the moving process less stressful and leave you feeling more confident about your choices.

In this guide you'll learn how to:

•Decide whether this is the right time for you to move
•Identify clear goals and expectations about your next home
•Get the best out of professionals helping you with your move
•Plan a calm, serene and productive move
•Avoid unnecessary stress, and feel content with your choices

What are you waiting for?

Get the book here – https://books2read.com/u/mV6ajM

Printed in Great Britain
by Amazon

77628113R00078